M000208583

BALLOON

A Fun and Easy Guide

to Making Balloon Animals,

Toys, and Games

SCULPTING

Second Edition

by
Dr. Dropo
(a.k.a. Bruce Fife)

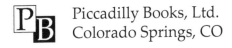

Piccadilly Books, Ltd.
Colorado Springs, CO

Copyright © 2009, 1994 Bruce Fife
All rights reserved. No part of this book may be reproduced in any
form without permission in writing from the publisher.

Illustrated by Ed Harris
Cover by Michael Donahue

Piccadilly Books, Ltd
P.O. Box 25203
Colorado Springs, CO 80936
www.piccadillybooks.com
info@piccadillybooks.com

Library of Congress Cataloging-in-Publication Data

Fife, Bruce, 1952-
 Balloon Sculpting/Bruce Fife.
 Rev. ed. of: Dr. Dropo's balloon sculpturing for
  beginners
 Includes references and index.
 ISBN 978-0-941599-83-2
 1. Balloon sculpture. I. Title.
TT926.F54 1988
745.594—dcl9   87-36151

Printed in the USA

CONTENTS

PREFACE 5
1 BALLOON BASICS 7
    Balloon Care   8
    Inflation   9
    Bubbles and Twists   14
    Character Aids   17

2 BALLOON ANIMALS 19
    The Basic Dog   19
    Dachshund   22
    Cocker Spaniel   23
    Giraffe   24
    Mouse   25
    Squirrel   26
    Horse   27
    Camel   27
    Rabbit   28
    Frog   29
    Mugwump   30
    Bumblebee   31
    Hummingbird   33
    Ladybug   33
    Swan   35
    Seal Balancing a Ball   37
    Penguin   38
    Brontosaurus   41
    French Poodle   43
    Cobra   47
    Snail   48
    Parrot   49
    Toucan   50
    Tyrannosaurus rex   52
    Monkey   54

Standing Dog   56
Alligator   58
The Extraterrestrial   59
Teddy Bear   61

3 **APPLE BALLOONS** **63**
Apple   63
Basket of Fruit   64
Bubble Baby   65
Chinaman   66
Baldheaded Man   67
Bubbles the Clown   68
Mr. Mustache   68
Troll   69
Smiley Face   69
Mr. Wrinkle   70
The Masked Marvel   71
More Balloon Guys   72

4 **BALLOON HATS** **73**
Basic Balloon Hat   73
Space Helmet   74
Animal Hats   76
Multiple Balloon Hat   79
Royal Crown   80

5 **GAMES AND TOYS** **81**
Airplane   81
High-Flyers   83
Tulip   84
Elephant Nose   86
Clown Nose   87
Pirate Sword   87
Bubble Gun   88
Fearless Freddy   90

INDEX **94**

PREFACE

My name is Bruce Fife. My friends call me Dr. Dropo. I'm a clown, a juggler, and a professor of balloonology. I teach classes in balloon science and other clown skills as well as demonstrate my balloon sculpting skills for countless children.

Being a clown balloonologist, I get the opportunity to make many balloon animals, especially at birthday parties. Balloons and parties go together like ice cream and cake. In my opinion, a party is not complete unless it has balloons, particularly sculptured balloons. These colorful bubbles create a festive atmosphere, provide a fun party activity, and make excellent gifts.

I began to learn the art of balloon sculpting several years ago when I started performing as "Dr. Dropo" at children's parties. I found that kids go wild over balloon animals and other balloon creations. Taking a limp, lifeless balloon and magically transforming it into a loveable bubbly animal fascinates and delights kids (and even adults).

My own three kids eagerly crowd around me every time I pull out a balloon. I'll make them each several figures. Then, with arms filled to capacity, scamper off to their rooms, deposit their treasure, and race back for more. Do they ever get tired of them . . . ? Not in the least. Over the years I've made thousands of the cute little creatures and still my kids' eyes light up with excitement every time they see me with a balloon.

This book was written for those who would like to share in the excitement of balloon sculpting, experience the thrill of turning a skinny piece of rubber into a cute loveable animal, and put smiles on children's faces (as well as on their own).

I have designed this book to teach beginners the basics of balloon sculpting, using easy-to-follow directions supplemented by clear illustrations to guide you every step of the way. The figures I've selected for this book include the ever-popular dog, as well as the rabbit, the frog, birds, funny hats, and even games, and toys. Although I can't claim all of the figures in this book to be my own original creations, all of the figures are favorites with kids and easy enough for any beginner to master with only a few minutes of practice.

Chapter 1

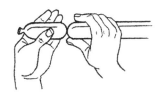

BALLOON BASICS

Like people, balloons come in all sizes and shapes. To make balloon figures from a single balloon you will need special balloons known as *pencil balloons* or *twistys*. These skinny balloons grow very long when inflated, allowing the balloon sculptor to twist them in an endless variety of shapes.

The most popular balloons used for sculpting are #260 pencil balloons. The number "2" in the code 260 refers to the diameter of the balloon when it's fully inflated. The "60" designates the length of the inflated balloon. All balloons can be identified by size, according to their code numbers. Round balloons are identified simply by their diameters (#6, #8, #10, etc.), and are rarely used in balloon sculpting. Most of the figures in this book can be made with the #260. I have also included a chapter which uses the *apple* (#321), *bee body* (#321), and *airship* (#312, #315, #330, #418, #524, plus others) balloons. Balloons that are used less frequently for sculpting are #280, #245, and #130.

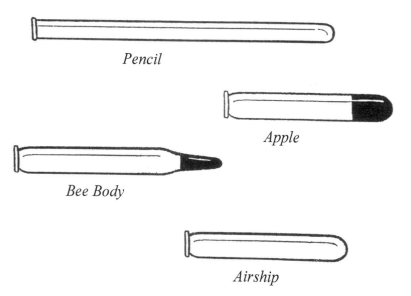

Pencil

Apple

Bee Body

Airship

These balloons can be obtained at novelty stores, such as magic shops and by mail order. Sometimes they can be found in toy stores. On pages 94 and 95 I have listed several mail order sources for balloons, in case you can't find them locally.

BALLOON CARE

In order to avoid unnecessary blowouts and to keep your balloon in good working order, you need to know about proper balloon maintenance.

Very little care is needed to keep your balloons in good working order. They never need washing or ironing; they need no food, oil, or periodic checkups. Being made of latex, however, balloons are perishable and will deteriorate with age. Heat, sunlight, and air, are the balloons worst enemies. If you keep the balloons out of the sunlight in an airtight container, and store them in a cool place they should remain usable for a year or more. I have had students come to my balloon sculpting classes with balloons over two years old, and they had no problems. But, if you buy a package of balloons and stick them on the dash board of your car on a hot summer day, don't expect them to last more than a day or so.

If you plan to store your balloons for a while, sprinkle a little corn starch or talcum powder on them. This prevents them from becoming sticky with age and prolongs their life.

With proper care and storage, balloons will last a long time. Storing them in a freezer or refrigerator normally isn't necessary.

As you work with balloons you will find, even with a fresh package of balloons, some variation in quality. Every package of balloons I've ever used has had its share of duds—balloons with tiny holes or thin spots that break when inflated. This is to be expected with any package of pencil balloons you buy, so don't be surprised to find a few bad ones.

INFLATION

If you are new to balloon sculpting you be surprised at the difficulty of inflating pencil balloons. Because the balloon's diameter is so small, blowing them up takes a good set of lungs.

To soften the balloon and make it easier to inflate, stretch it a few times. But be careful not to overstretch it; a balloon stretched to its elastic limits will develop lumps when inflated. A lumpy balloon will make the animal you create look deformed.

To inflate the balloon, use your cheek muscles to start a bubble. Once a bubble is started, take a deep breath and use your chest and diaphragm muscles to inflate the rest of the balloon with one continuous blow.

Some people like to pull the nipple end of the balloon as they blow. This action tends to encourage the air into the balloon, making inflation somewhat easier. If you try this, don't be overzealous. If you pull too much or too fast, you'll make inflation more difficult.

When you first try to inflate the skinny #260 balloons, you may experience some dizziness. But with a week or two of light practice your lung strength should increase and you will no longer be troubled with this feeling.

If after stretching the balloon you still have trouble inflating it, don't give up; there's another method that makes putting air in a balloon as easy as tooting on a whistle. The secret? An air pump. That's right—almost any hand pump can be used, as long as the nozzle of the balloon can fit on it. I used an ordinary foot pump when I first started as a balloon sculptor. Pumps can be purchased at stores which sell bicycles or sporting goods. Hand pumps designed especially for balloons are also available. You can find pumps at your local novelty shop or in mail order catalogs. See the appendix for a listing of mail order companies who sell balloon pumps and supplies.

Another advantage to using a pump is that you can inflate a limitless number of balloons without killing yourself. For a clown surrounded by a mob of kids anxiously waiting for each creation, a pump comes in mighty handy.

How much air should you put into the balloon? Rarely will you ever inflate it fully. Usually you will leave an inch or two uninflated at the very end. As you tie off the balloon and begin to twist bubbles, the air in the balloon will be forced toward the end, gradually inflating the tail. If you don't leave this tail, the end of the balloon will stretch tighter and tighter, making it difficult to twist the bubbles and increase the chances of popping.

The type of animal you make determines how long this tail should be. A dog, for instance, needs only two inches uninflated. A mouse needs six or seven inches.

Balloon Busting

Sometimes when you blow up a balloon, that's exactly what happens—it blows up! I've noticed an inherent fear of blowouts, especially in beginners. They twist the bubbles very gingerly as if expecting them to explode at any second. Some clinch their teeth tightly, as if that would prevent the balloon from popping. Others close their eyes, tense up, and contort their faces, stretching them more than

the balloon. I even find myself doing this at times. But never, never, never, in all the time I have been working with balloons and in all the classes I've taught, never has anybody ever been mortally wounded by a popped balloon.

I have yet to see, a drop of blood, a dislocated shoulder, a blister, a bruise, or any other physical injury caused by such a mishap.

Exploding balloons are a part of the balloon sculptor's experience. Like taxes, there is no way around them. You can be as careful as a nitroglycerine salesmen, but all balloons are not made equal. Some will pop without apparent reason, no matter how careful you are. I've only been hit in the face once, that I can recall, with a piece of exploding balloon. It left no disfiguring scar and I lived to tell about it, so don't worry about popping your bubbles.

Most pencil balloons are surprisingly resilient, especially the #260E variety. They can withstand a lot of twisting, tugging, stretching, and shoving without breaking.

To cut down on the number of balloons that will pop and to make the balloon easier to work with, I recommend that you treat the balloon like a little baby after it had a meal. I don't mean change its diaper—but to "burp it." Before tying off the end, let out a little air, just enough to make it "burp." This will make the balloon softer and easier to work with.

Tying Off the Balloon

There are several ways to tie off a balloon. Any method that works is acceptable. I have two methods I like best. Experiment with both and see what one you prefer, or use a method of your own.

First Method. Hold the balloon between the thumb and first finger of one hand, as shown in the illustration below. With the other hand pull the nozzle down and around the first finger. Tuck the nozzle under the loop and pull it through.

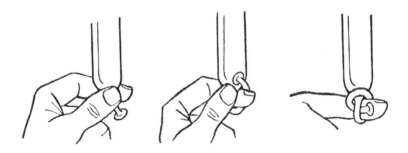

Second Method. This method works well for those who have thin finders. My fingers are on the thin side, so I usually tie my balloons this way.

Start by holding the balloon between the thumb and first finger, as shown below. Wrap the nozzle around the ends of the first two fingers. Insert the nozzle under the loop in the space between the fingers. Pull on the nozzle, making a knot while slipping the fingers out.

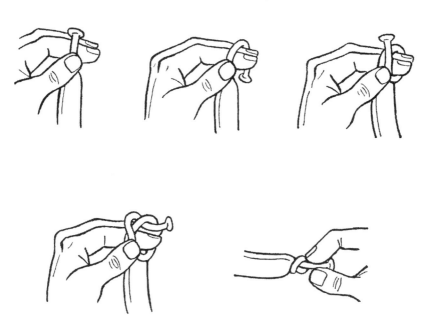

BUBBLES AND TWISTS

Balloon figures are created by twisting off various sized bubbles and arranging them into specific patterns. The bubbles are made by twisting the balloon in opposite directions. Twist each bubble at least two complete revolutions so they won't unravel as you work.

14

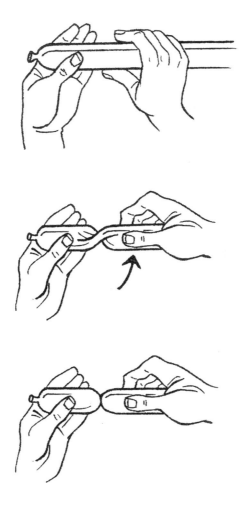

After twisting off each bubble, make sure to continue to hold them, or they will untwist. Only after you have made an connecting twist can you let go. Connecting twists are usually used to connect two or more bubbles. As an example, twist out three two-inch bubbles (1, 2, and 3). The remaining portion of the balloon will be bubble 4.

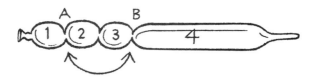

Make sure you twist each bubble in the same direction or they will untwist in your hand. Connect point A with point B (see illustration). While holding bubbles 4 and 1, twist together bubbles 3 and 2 as shown below.

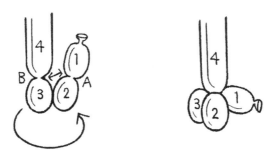

This is the basic type of twist that you'll use to make connections. Another type of connecting twist, called a *loop twist*, is also important. A loop twist is simply a bubble connected to itself (see the following illustration).

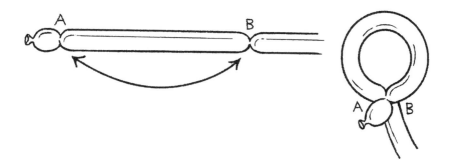

Loop twists with large bubbles make good hats. Loop twisting small bubbles make good ears or wings for animal figures, and are sometimes referred to as *ear twists*.

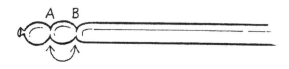

CHARACTER AIDS

Markings such as mouth and eyes can give your creation a personality, thus making it more realistic. Most all figures you make will take on a more recognizable and lifelike appearance with the addition of these character aids. Certain animals may require distinguishing marks such as whiskers, spots, and strips to make them recognizable.

Markings can do wonders in bringing your figure to life, but don't overdo it! Usually the fewest marks you can make are the best. Too much ink distracts from the balloon itself, and can even look ugly. For most figures just adding eyes and/or a mouth is all that is needed.

Not all pens will not write on the latex balloons, and some that do, don't look good. I have discovered the best type of pen is a permanent felt tip marker such as Sanford's Sharpie. These pens give a nice solid black line that I can make either fat or thin, depending on how I use it.

Balloons come in a variety of colors, adding to the character of each creation. Although figures can be made using any color, some animals look better when made with certain colors. A swan looks best if made with a white balloon; a bee is more recognizable if you use a yellow balloon; a ladybug looks best in red or orange.

The fact that you can make most figures out of any color adds variety to your creations. Even if you can only make two or three different animals, each creation can be unique when you use different colors and make different markings and expressions.

Chapter 2

BALLOON ANIMALS

Let's start with the all time easiest and most popular balloon creature—the annelid. What's an annelid? You'll recognize it when we're finished.

Inflate a balloon about a foot or so and tie it off (the exact amount of air for this creature is not important). Now take a pin or a ball point pen and make a hole, popping the balloon. You will be left with a long, scrawny piece of rubber which resembles an annelid. (If you don't recognize what an annelid is, it's a worm!)

Worms aren't that popular with kids, but balloonologists love to make them—they make them all time almost as if by accident.

There is an endless variety of methods used to make worms. Some are very complex, involving many bubbles and twists before popping, but the end result is always the same—the worm.

As a new balloonologist, you too will learn to master the worm, and it will soon become one of your most often repeated creations.

Now that I've discussed one of the unavoidable mishaps of balloon sculpting, let's look at some serious creations.

THE DOG

The dog is a basic balloon figure. It is easy to make, and is the most requested by children. Once you have learned how to make the basic dog, making many of the other balloon animals will be easy.

To make the dog, start by inflating a pencil balloon all the way to the end except for about two or three inches. "Burp" it to let a little bit of air escape, and then tie off the nozzle end. Twist off three three-inch bubbles (1, 2, and 3) and twist connect them at points A and B.

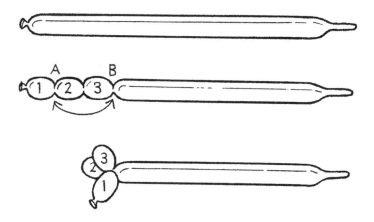

Twist off three more bubbles of the same size (4, 5, and 6) and connect points C and D.

20

Make an eight-inch bubble (7) for the body and twist off two additional bubbles (8 and 9) the same size as bubbles 5 and 6. You will be left with only a small bubble (10) at the end, to be used as the tail.

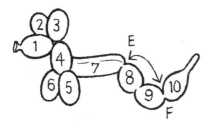

Twist connect points E and F. Arrange the bubbles in a realistic position and finish by marking in eyes and mouth.

Your first attempt at making the dog may have resulted in something a little different from the dog pictured here. However, with a little practice your figures will improve.

The steps used to make the dog are basically the same for many other types of animals. By varying the size of the bubbles on the dog's body, you can create other animals. I will show several variations in the following pages. As we go along the figures will start to deviate from the basic dog shape. Some of these figures will be very simple for you to make, while others will require a bit more practice to master.

DACHSHUND

As far as hounds are concerned the dachshund is a low down dog. But it makes a good family dog because all the members of the family can pet it at the same time.

The sequence for making the dachshund is the same as that just described for the dog. The only difference is that you lengthen the body and shorten the legs slightly.

Connect the bubbles as shown below. Draw in eyes and mouth to make it complete.

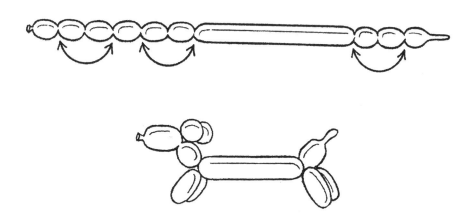

COCKER SPANIEL

This is another simple variation of the basic dog. You start by making the dog as describe previously. To turn the basic dog into the cocker spaniel all you need to do is rearrange the dogs head and ear bubbles.

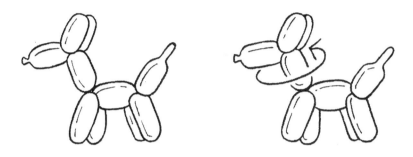

Twist the head and ears upside down as shown above. From this position, spread the two ear bubbles and push the nose bubble down halfway between them. Do the same thing with the neck bubble, pushing it halfway between the ears so that it touches the nose bubble (see the illustration below).

Finally, position the head, ears, and neck bubbles until they look right. The cocker spaniel is now complete.

GIRAFFE

What do giraffes have that no other animal has?. . . Little giraffes of course.

The giraffe is made by lengthening the neck on the basic dog figure. Legs are also lengthened and ears shortened. The addition of semi-square spots on the neck makes the giraffe easily recognizable.

MOUSE

   The mouse is one of my favorite balloon animals. It's quick and easy to make, and kids love it.

   The bubbles in the mouse are all significantly smaller than the dog's. Since the bubbles are small, the balloon should be inflated no more than about eight inches. This will leave a long uninflated portion of the balloon at the nipple end, which will become the the mouse's tail.

   Twist off a two- to three-inch bubble to form the head. All other bubbles except the body will be one-inchers. The body bubble will be two to three inches long. Draw in eyes, mouth, and whickers to finish (see the illustration below).

SQUIRREL

I'm nutty about this animal, but my friends tell me I'm just nutty.

The squirrel is made with bubbles, not much larger then those in the mouse. The big difference is the tail; for the squirrel it is fully inflated.

Begin by inflating a balloon fully except for about two inches. Twist off and connect the bubble just as you would the mouse.

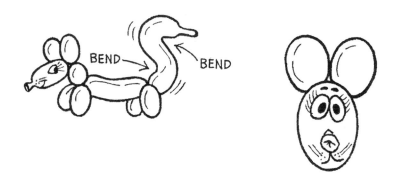

Shaping the tail helps to make the squirrel lifelike. To put a permanent curve in the balloon, bend it in the direction you want it to curve and squeeze the sides a couple of times. The tail will retain a squirrel-like curve. For the final touch, add a squirrel face like the one pictured here.

HORSE

The horse, the original oatsmobile, will have slightly longer legs and neck than the dog. The ears should be made from small bubbles. Marking a mane on the back of the horse's neck helps distinguish it from the dog. You might even add a little saddle on the horse's back.

CAMEL

Before I got into the balloon business I was a used camel salesman. But I lost my job because of illness and fatigue— my boss was sick and tired of me.

The horse can be transformed into a camel by bending and shaping some of the bubbles. Start by making the horse. Bend and squeeze the horse's head, neck, and body (just as you did with the squirrel's tail) in the directions shown below. You now have a camel.

RABBIT

I learned how to make these rabbits at my last job, where I worked as a rabbit breeder—it really kept me hopping.

To create a rabbit, give the basic dog figure longer ears and hind legs, and make the neck slightly smaller.

After twisting off all bubbles and making all connections, push the two front legs between the back legs, putting the rabbit into a sitting position. Usually the rabbit is easily recognizable at this stage, but adding a bunny-like face (use a face like the squirrel's) it turns into a cute bubbly rabbit.

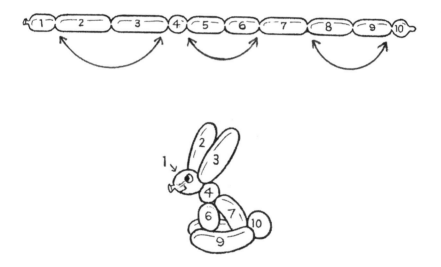

How can you find a lost rabbit? Simple, just make a noise like a carrot.

FROG

The frog is made in much the same way as the rabbit, with some notable differences. The first four bubbles combine to form the frog's head.

Inflate the balloon fully except for about two inches. Start by making a one-inch bubble (1). Make two three-inch bubbles (2 and 3), these will be the frog's eyes. Connect points A and B. For the mouth make an eight-inch bubble (4) and make a loop twist, connecting points B and C.

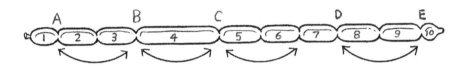

Push bubbles 2 and 3 up through the center of bubble 4 to create the frog's head (see the illustration below). This is easier if you roll bubble 4 over bubbles 2 and 3.

Twist off two three-inch bubbles (5 and 6) and connect them as indicated. These will be the frog's front legs. Twist off another bubble (7) a little larger than bubbles 5 and 6 but no bigger than four inches. This will be the frog's body. Divide the remaining bubble in half to form bubbles 8 and 9. Twist off a one-inch bubble (10) at the tail end of bubble 9.

Connect points D and E to form the frog's back legs. Tuck the two front legs (bubbles 5 and 6) between the back legs, as you did for the rabbit. Adding a face to the frog makes it easily recognizable.

MUGWUMP

"What's a mugwump?" you ask. A mugwump is an animal that sits on a fence with its mug on one side and its wump on the other.

Since this is an imaginary creature, you can make it look like most anything you want, this is my version.

Inflate a pencil balloon, leaving two inches uninflated. Follow the steps for making the standard dog figure, using

a four-inch long bubble for the nose, and leave a long squirrel-type tail. I also make the front legs shorter than the back ones. Put a bend in the nose and tail, as shown, and draw in a face.

Although the mugwump doesn't represent any real animal, kids enjoy it because it's so cute.

BUMBLEBEE

We now depart from the basic dog figure and begin making figures which have different shapes. Several winged creations can be made using just four bubbles.

The bumblebee is a simple little balloon figure kids adore. For appearance's sake a yellow balloon works best. Inflate the balloon leaving a three-inch tail at the end. Burp it and tie it off. Make a two-inch bubble (1) below the knot and hold it. Bend the entire balloon in half as shown on the following page. Twist off a three-inch bubble at the tail end of the balloon. Connect points A and B. Bubble 1 becomes the bee's head and bubble 4 becomes the bee's body with the tail as the stinger.

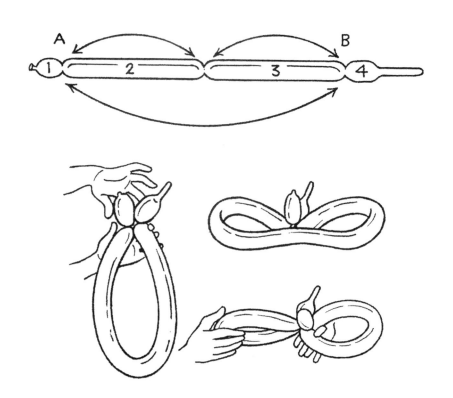

To make the wings, position the head and body midway between the center bubble (as shown above). This will split the balloon loop in half to form to equal sized wings. To lock the wings in place twist one of the wings around a couple of times.

Adjust the wings and body as shown in the drawing below. Draw eyes and mouth on the head, and stripes on the body.

Where do bumblebees come from?. . . Stingapore.

HUMMINGBIRD

Some birds sing, others whistle, but a hummingbird hums—why is that . . . ? Because he doesn't know the words.

The humming bird is made much the same way as the bumblebee. Make all of the bubbles and connecting twists just as you would the bumblebee.

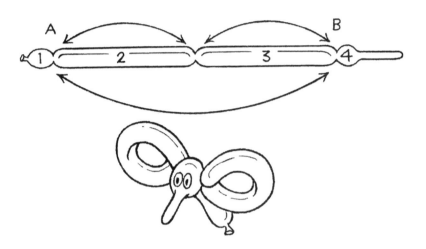

You have what looks like the bumblebee. The difference is you will reverse the head and the tail. Bubble 4 becomes the head and bubble 1 becomes the tail as shown in the illustration. Position the bubbles and draw in a couple of eyes to finish.

LADYBUG

Flying insects bug some people more than others. Some people shoo them, while others just let them run around barefoot.

The ladybug is one of the cutest little balloon figures I've seen. Although it uses only four bubbles, it's a little harder to make than some of the others you've worked on so far. The tricky part about the ladybug is making the small loop twists (ear twists). These twists get tight, and it may take you a little practice to master. Ear twists are easier to make if the balloon is softened by releasing a little extra air before tying off the balloon.

Orange, red, and yellow balloons look best, but any color can be used. Inflate the balloon *at least* eight inches. Don't worry about the length of the tail. Twist off one two-inch bubble (1), a three-inch bubble (2), a one-inch bubble (3), and another three-inch bubble (4), and hold them.

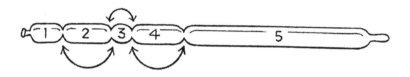

Ear twist bubbles 2, 3, and 4. Twist bubble 3 first, then 2, and finally 4.

Make a small hole in bubble 5 and release the air. This bubble will deflate, but the others will remain air tight. Use a pair of scissors to cut the deflated portion of the balloon off.

Arrange the bubbles to look like the figure shown below. Bubble 1 becomes the body, bubble 3 the head, and bubbles 2 and 4 the wings. Add spots to the bug's back and draw in a face.

SWAN

What did the swan say when it laid a square egg? "Ouch!"

The swan is one of the classic balloon figures most all balloon sculptors have in their repertoire. Its long slender neck and simple twists make it ideal for balloon sculpting. Many versions exist, but the one I show you here is my favorite.

Inflate a pencil balloon fully except for about three or four inches. Make a one-inch bubble (1), followed by two six-inch bubbles (2 and 3). Connect the bubbles at points A and B.

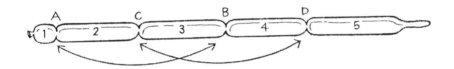

Twist off bubble 4. Bubbles 2, 3, and 4 should all be the same length. Connect points C and D by simply pushing point D between bubbles 2 and 3. You don't need to make any twists for this connection (see illustration).

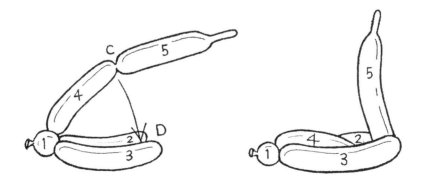

The remaining bubble will become the swan's head and neck. Making the head requires a trick that may take a little practice. Bend the nipple over and grab the balloon about an inch below the top, as show in the illustration. Grabbing the neck of the balloon with both hands, squeeze tightly, forcing air up into the tip. For best results, squeeze only once but squeeze hard.

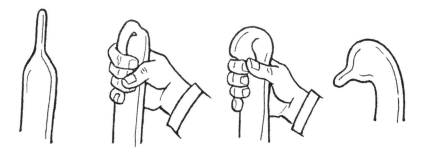

Bend and shape the swan's neck into a natural curve. A pair of eyes is all the marking you need to finish this figure.

SEAL BALANCING A BALL

This is a seal-ly (silly) balloon figure that you're sure to enjoy.

The seal is made very much like the swan. Inflate the balloon leaving about three or four inches in the tail. Twist off bubbles 1, 2, 3, and 4, and connect them as shown, just as if making the swan's body.

Twist off two one-inch bubbles 5 and 6, and connect as shown to form the front fins.

To make the ball on the seal's nose, with one hand hold bubble 7 and half of the *uninflated* portion of the seal's nose. With the other hand

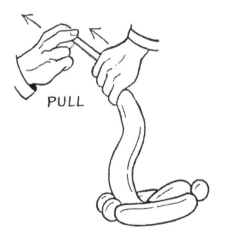

grab just the tip of the uninflated nose and stretch it by pulling it several times. This stretching will weaken the end of the balloon so that air can form a bubble at this end without inflating the rest.

After stretching the tip, hold bubble 7 and the unstretched portion of the seal's nose and squeeze, forcing air into the tip. You'll end up with a small bubble joined by a short section of uninflated balloon, which looks like a ball on the seal's nose.

Finish by shaping the seal's neck in the proper position.

Put your seal of approval on this one by clapping your hands and say "Arf."

PENGUIN

The penguin is a very cute figure and makes a nice companion for the seal.

Inflate a pencil balloon leaving a four-inch tail and tie it off. Twist off an eight-inch bubble (1) and two six-inch bubbles (2 and 3). These will form the penguin's head and body. Twist connect points A and B.

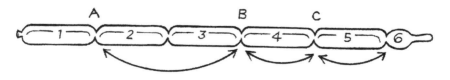

Take the remaining bubble and twist it in half to form two bubbles (4 and 5). Fold bubble 4 in half, as shown below, and connect it to itself with a loop twist (connect points B and C). At the very end of bubble 5 twist off a one-inch bubble (6). While holding bubble 6 so it doesn't untwist, fold bubble 5 in half and loop twist it like you did with bubble 4. Bubbles 4 and 5 form the penguin's feet and bubble 6 becomes it's tail.

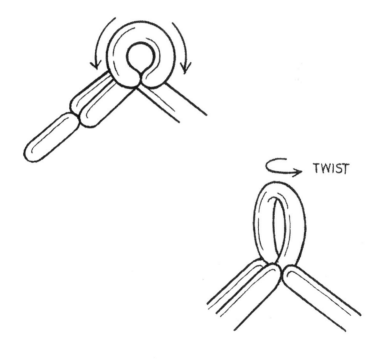

TWIST

Now take bubble 1 and twist off a one-inch bubble at the nozzle end and hold it. Spread bubbles 2 and 3 apart as shown on the following page. While spreading these bubbles, push part of bubble 1 between them. Don't push

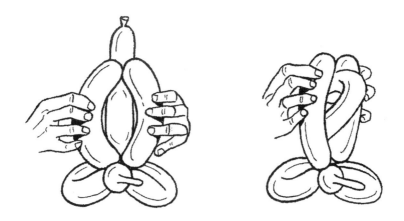

bubble 1 all the way through; just a couple of inches below the nozzle bubble. The small bubble at the nozzle end of bubble 1 becomes the penguin's beak and the lower end becomes it's belly. Adjust the bubbles to the shape shown below and you're finished.

BRONTOSAURUS

What animal makes noise when it sleeps? A dino-snore. Dinosaurs are always popular with kids. This Brontosaurus will make you the hit at any party.

Inflate a balloon, leaving a three-inch tail at the end, and tie it off. Start by making a seven-inch bubble (1) and two three-inch bubbles (2 and 3). Connect points A and B. The first three bubbles will form the head, neck, and front legs. We will come back to them later.

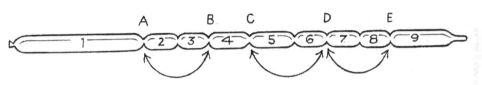

Make three four-inch bubble (4, 5, and 6). Connect points C and D.

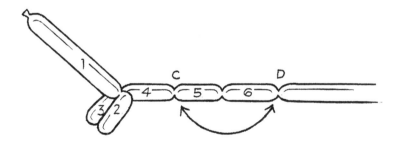

Spread bubbles 4 and 5 apart and push (or rather roll) bubble 3 in between them and all the way to the other side (see the illustration below). These three bubble form the figure's chunky body.

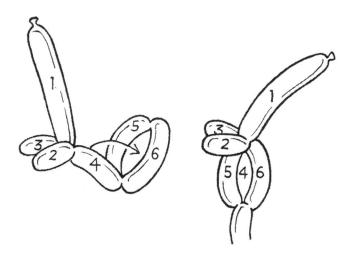

Make two three-inch bubbles (7 and 8). Connect points D and E to form the back legs.

Go back to bubble 1 and bend the top of it, as shown on the right, and squeeze the sides a few times (just as you did with the camel). This will put in a permanent curve into the neck to form the head.

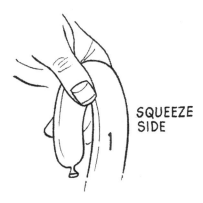

SQUEEZE SIDE

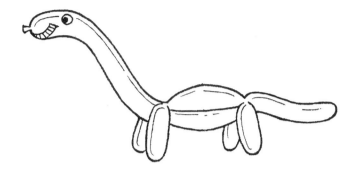

The remaining bubble (9) becomes the tail. If there is any uninflated portion of the tail remaining, squeeze the air to inflate the entire bubble. Bend and shape it as desired. Draw in eyes and a mouth.

FRENCH POODLE

I call my dog a miniature poodle. The miniature (minute you) turn your back he does a poodle.

The poodle is much like the basic dog figure, with some notable differences. It is actually one of the more difficult figures described in this book. It is so cute it will become one of your favorites.

Inflate the balloon fully except for about five inches. Release some air to soften the balloon and tie it off. Twist off two three-inch bubbles (1 and 2), a one-inch bubble (3), and another three-inch bubble (4). Keep hold of these bubbles so they don't untwist. Holding all these bubbles without letting any of them unwind is a little tricky at first, but you will get the hang of it with a little practice. Make your first connection at points A and B to form the poodle's head.

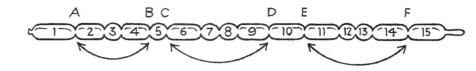

Make a three-inch bubble (6), two one-inch bubbles (7 and 8), and another three-inch bubble (9). When you make bubbles 7 and 8 twist them a few extra times so that they don't untwist. Connect them at points C and D to form the front legs.

Make two three-inch bubbles (10 and 11), two one-inch bubbles (12 and 13), and another three-inch bubble (14). Connect points E and F to form the back legs.

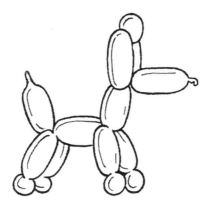

After you finish making all the bubbles and connecting twists, shaping the head and tail gives this figure it's distinctive poodle appearance.

Return to the first bubble to finish the head. Fold bubble 1 in half and push the nozzle end between bubbles 2 and 4 (see illustration). Push the nose (1) about halfway through the ears (2 and 4). Squeeze the ears lightly and at the same time give a gentle tug on the knot to lengthen the nose a bit (see illustration).

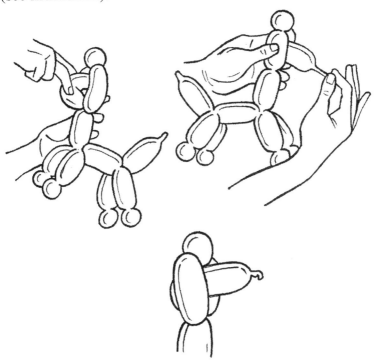

Now go to the tail. With one hand, hold bubble 15 and half of the uninflated portion of the tail. With the other hand grab the tip of the tail and stretch it by pulling it several times. This stretching will weaken the end of the balloon so air can form a bubble there without inflating the rest of the tail.

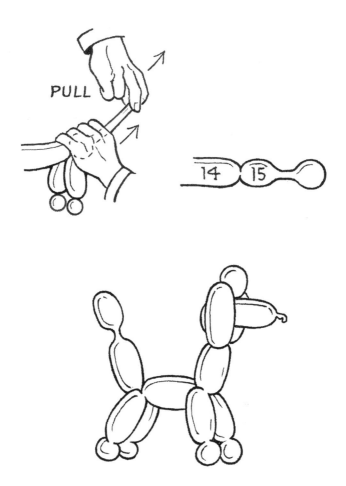

Hold bubble 15 and the unstretched portion of the tail and squeeze. A bubble should develop at the end of the tail. This is the same procedure you used earlier to make the ball on the seal's nose.

Another way to make this bubble is to put the end of the uninflated end in your mouth and suck the air into that part of the balloon. A small bubble will develop in your mouth, and your tail is finished. Some people prefer this method over the first one, but it leaves your poodle's tail wet and a rubbery taste in your mouth.

COBRA

A snake-charmer married an undertaker. As a wedding present they received a pair of towels marked "Hiss" and "Hearse."

You can become a snake-charmer with this cobra. It requires only four bubbles and is easy to make.

Inflate the balloon leaving a one-inch tail. Twist off one two-inch bubble (1) and two four-inch bubbles (2 and 3). Connect points A and B.

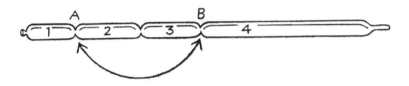

Spread bubbles 2 and 3 and push the top part of bubble 4 between them. Give the snake's body a coiled appearance by bending and shaping it.

Finish by marking in a couple of beady eyes and nostrils.

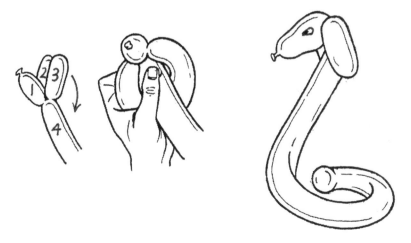

SNAIL

This is another simple balloon figure.

Inflate a balloon leaving a two-inch tail. Twist off a three-inch bubble (1), and two one-inch bubbles (2, and 3). Connect points A and B.

Make two seven-inch bubbles and connect points C and D.

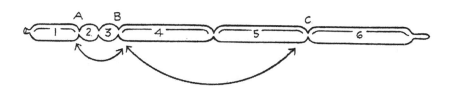

Squeeze bubble 6 so that the air fills up the balloon all the way to the tail. Starting at the tail end, roll the bubble up into a coil. Wedge the coiled bubble between bubbles 4 and 5 as shown. Adjust bubbles 1, 2, and 3 to look like the illustration below.

PARROT

The parrot is one of my favorite balloon animals. Since many parrots have green feathers make this figure using a green balloon.

Inflate the balloon leaving a two-inch tail. To form the parrot's head start by twisting off three two-inch bubbles. Connect points A and B. Push the nozzle on bubble 1 in between bubbles 2 and 3. Bubble 1 will become the parrot's beak (see illustration).

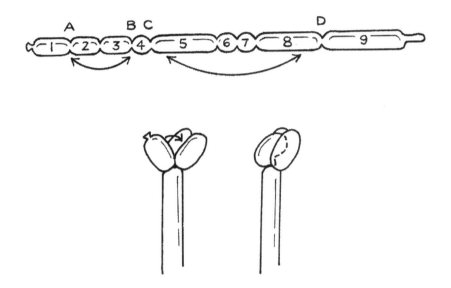

Twist off one one-inch bubble (4), one five-inch bubble (5), two one-inch bubbles (6 and 7), and another five-inch bubble (8). Connect points C and D. Bubbles 5 and 8 become the parrot's wings and bubbles 6 and 7 it's feet.

Pull the wings apart slightly and push the nipple end of the remaining bubble (9) between them. Push all of bubble 9 through the wings except for about five inches. Bubble 9 forms the parrot's chest and tail. Position the bubble as shown.

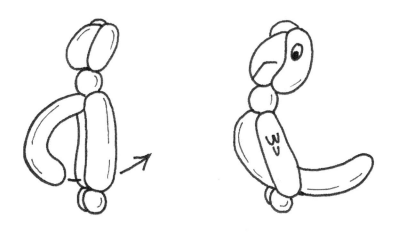

You can draw in a couple of eyes and put a mouth on the beak. You could also put a few feathers on the wings. Don't put too many feathers on, just enough to give definition to the wings.

TOUCAN

The toucan is made similar to parrot. The biggest difference is the toucan's distinctive large beak. These are naturally colorful birds so you may want to try using a brightly colored balloon.

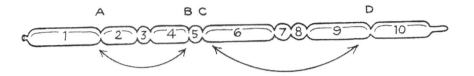

Inflate the balloon leaving a three-inch tail. Twist off one five-inch balloon (1), a two-inch balloon (2), one one-inch balloon (3), and another two-inch balloon (4). Connect points A and B. Bend bubble 1 in half and push the knot in between bubbles 2, 3, and 4. Shape bubble 1 into the toucan's beak as shown.

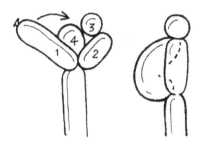

Twist off one one-inch bubble (5), one five-inch bubble (6), two one-inch bubbles (7 and 8), and another five-inch bubble (9). Connect points C and D.

Push about half of bubble 10 between bubbles 6 and 9. The nipple end becomes the toucan's tail and the other end it's chest. Position the natural bend of the balloon so that it curves downward.

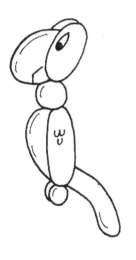

You can put on eyes, mouth, and a few feathers to finish.

TYRANNOSAURUS REX

What do you get if two dinosaurs crash into each other? Tyrannosaurus wrecks (rex).

This ferocious king of dinosaurs is a big hit with kids.

Inflate a balloon leaving a two-inch tail. Make a two and a half-inch bubble (1), a three-inch bubble (2), and two half-inch bubbles (3 and 4). Holding all bubbles connect points B and C first.

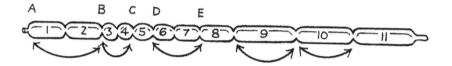

Next connect point A, the nozzle of bubble 1, to point B. Simply wrap the nozzle around point B. Pressure from the other balloons will keep it in place. Position bubble 1 beneath bubble 2 as shown below.

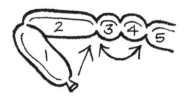

Make three two-inch bubbles (5, 6, and 7) and connect points D and E. These form the upper arms. Make a three-inch bubble (8) for the body, and five-inch bubble (9). Loop twist bubble 9 to form one leg. Make another five-inch bubble (10) and loop twist it to form the other leg. The remaining bubble (11) becomes the tail.

To straighten out Rex's body tuck the ends of bubbles 5 (neck) and 8 (body) between bubbles 6 and 7 (arms).

Draw in a pair of piercing eyes and sharp teeth if you desire.

MONKEY

Inflate the balloon leaving a three-inch tail. Make a one-inch bubble (1), a half-inch bubble (2), followed by four one-inch bubbles (3, 4, 5, and 6). The trickiest part of this figure is keeping all of these bubbles in your hand without letting any of them unwind.

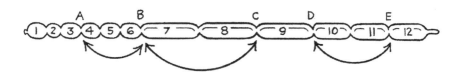

Keep hold of bubbles 1, 2, and 3, and connect points A and B. Now, push bubble 1 between bubbles 4, 5, and 6. It is a tight squeeze, but if you roll bubbles 4 and 6 over bubble 1 as you push it in, the process is easier. Pull bubble 1 all the way through. Bubble 1 becomes the back of the monkey's head. Bubble 2 becomes it's nose and bubble 3 it's mouth and lips.

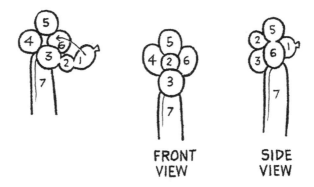

FRONT VIEW   SIDE VIEW

54

Twist off two five-inch bubbles (7 and 8) and connect points B and C. These become the monkey's arms.

Make another five-inch bubble (9) followed by two three-inch bubbles (10 and 11). Connect points D and E.

Push the top part of bubble 9 in between bubbles 7 and 8 to form the monkey's chest, as shown below. Bend the tail upward as shown. Finish with a few simple facial markings.

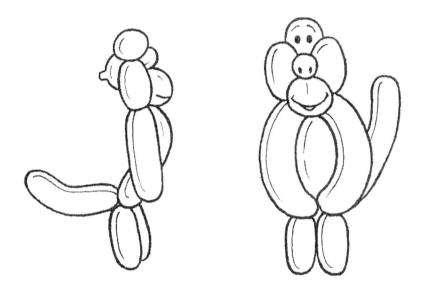

I'm stronger than Tarzan the Ape Man. I can beat my chest without yelling!

STANDING DOG

You should have noticed by now that all of the dogs described in this book as well as many of the other balloon animals will not stand up if you place them on a table. This is a common characteristic with most balloon figures. The dog you will make now is one that can stand on its on four feet. It is a little tricker than the other dogs because it involves cutting the balloon with a pair of scissors. If you make the bubble correctly even after you cut it the balloon will remain air tight.

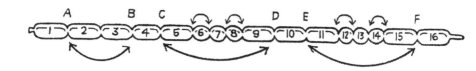

Blow up a balloon leaving five inches uninflated. Twist off three two-inch bubbles (1, 2, and 3). Connect points A and B.

Twist off two two-inch bubbles (4 and 5), three half-inch bubbles (6, 7, and 8), and one more two-inch bubble (9). The small half-inch bubbles have a tendency to untwist so, when you're making them, give them an extra twist or two. Connect points C and D.

Twist off two two-inch bubbles (10 and 11), three half-inch bubbles (12, 13, and 14), and one two-inch bubble (15). Connect points E and F.

Now comes the tricky part. Ear twist bubbles 6, 8, 12, and 14. The ear twists will become so tight that you

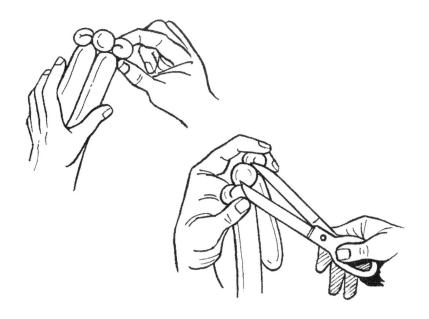

can cut bubbles 7 and 13 without popping the balloon. When you cut these bubbles make sure you gently hold with your fingers the bubbles on either side. If you don't hold these bubbles the shock of the popping bubble may unravel one or both of the bubbles next to them. After cutting bubbles 7 and 13 the dog's legs spread out and you can stand it up on the table to admire.

ALLIGATOR

Why do alligators eat raw meat? Because they don't know how to cook.

This is another figure which requires cutting. Inflate a balloon leaving a three-inch tail. Make two three-inch bubbles (1 and 2), three half-inch bubbles (3, 4, and 5), and another three-inch bubble (6). Connect points A and B. This will form the alligator's head and front legs.

To make the rest of the alligator twist off one six-inch bubble (7), one three-inch bubble (8), three half-inch bubbles (9, 10, and 11), and another three-inch bubble (12). Connect points C and D.

Ear twist bubbles 3, 5, 9, and 11. Cut bubbles 4 and 10.

Position the bubbles as shown. Draw in eyes, nostrils, and mouth.

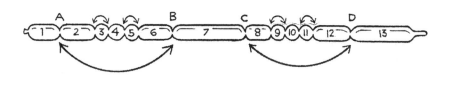

THE EXTRATERRESTRIAL

Here is a cute little creature from outer space that every kid will enjoy.

Inflate a balloon leaving a five-inch tail. Twist off a two-inch bubble (1) and six small bubbles, each a little less than one-inch (2, 3, 4, 5, 6, and 7). Hold on to each bubble so they don't unwind. Connect points A and B. Push bubble 1 in between the ring of small bubbles as shown. This forms the top of the creature's head.

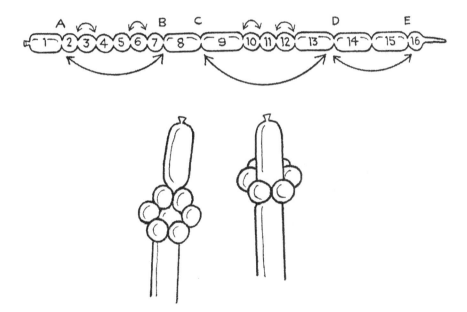

Make a two-inch bubble (8), a three-inch bubble (9), three one-inch bubbles (10, 11, and 12), and another three-inch bubble (13). Connect points C and D.

To make the legs, divide the remaining bubble in half and twist off two bubbles (14 and 15). Make a one-inch bubble at the very end (16). Connect points D and E.

Ear twist bubbles 3, 6, 10, and 12. Bubbles 3 and 6 will become the creature's ears and bubbles 10 and 12 its hands. Cut bubble 11 and open up the alien's arms.

Finish by marking in the eyes, mouth, and nose as shown. Awesome! You can almost here it say, "Take me to your leader."

Although this figure makes a funny little alien, space creatures can be any configuration. You can easily create your own. In fact, I create space creatures all the time when I make other figures. If the giraffe I happen to be working on ends up looking more like an anteater, or if a bubble accidently pops, the figure instantly becomes a "creature from outer space." These impromptu aliens are almost as popular as ordinary animals. The creature I describe here, however, has been my most popular extraterrestrial.

TEDDY BEAR

The teddy bear is the most difficult figure described in this book. It contains 18 bubbles and requires some cutting. I have included it just to give you a challenge. If you can make this figure successfully then you are ready to tackle advanced figures like Snoopy juggling three balls while riding a unicycle.*

Inflate a balloon leaving a five-inch tail. Twist off a three-inch bubble (1), a two-inch bubble (2), a half-inch bubble (3), a one and a half-inch bubble (4), another half-inch bubble (5), and another two-inch bubble (6). Connect points A and B. Ear twist bubbles 3 and 5. These become the bear's ears. Push the nozzle end of bubble 1 halfway through bubbles 2 and 6. This becomes the bear's snout.

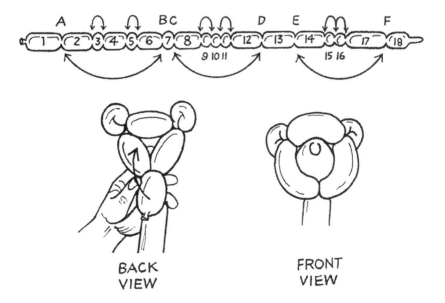

BACK VIEW

FRONT VIEW

*Believe it or not, the balloon figure Snoopy juggling three balls while riding a unicycle can be made. Booklets describing how to make advanced figures like this can be obtained from Piccadilly Books, P.O. Box 25203, Colorado Springs, CO 80936, USA. Write and ask for a free catalog.

Make a one-inch bubble (7), a two-inch bubble (8), three half-inch bubbles (9, 10, and 11), and another two-inch bubble (12). Connect points C and D.

Make two two-inch bubbles (13 and 14), two half-inch bubbles (15 and 16), and another two-inch bubble (17). Connect points E and F.

Ear twist bubbles 9, 11, 15, and 16. Cut bubbles 10. Position bubbles as shown below.

Have you ever hunted bear? I haven't, but I once went fishing in my shorts.

Chapter 3

APPLE BALLOONS

Apple balloons are much shorter than pencil balloons and a bit wider, so they're easier to inflate. They come in a variety of colors, most commonly red, yellow, green, and light blue. Their most distinguishing characteristic is the dark green nipple, which forms the stem when making the apple.

Although I use apple balloons in the following descriptions, you can make these figures using bee body or airship balloons as well.

APPLE

Use one apple balloon to make this classic. Inflate the balloon about halfway. With your finger, push the nozzle into the balloon and all the way into the nipple end.

Grab both the nipple and the nozzle with the fingers of your other hand and remove your finger. Now make an apple twist by turning the bubble as you hold the two ends securely. This action will lock the nozzle and nipple together forming an apple-shaped bubble.

You can make different types of apples by changing the color: red apples, green and yellow apples, and even blue apples (yum yum).

BASKET OF FRUIT

A basket of fruit can be created by making an assortment of red, green, and yellow apples, combined with bananas and grapes.

The bananas are made from yellow pencil balloons. Use only eight or nine inches of a balloon and put a banana-like curve in it.

The grapes are made from red, yellow, or purple pencil balloons. Inflate the balloon and twist off a several of small bubbles in a row. Twist connect the bubbles to form a bunch of grapes.

Put all the balloon fruit in a basket or bowl, and you have a decorative arrangement. Anyone care for a snack?

BUBBLE BABY

Apple balloons were produced originally to make rubber apples, but they can easily be transformed into bubble babies and balloon guys. Many variations are possible; here are a few to get you started.

Making the bubble baby and all the other balloon guys is very similar to making the rubber apple. The major difference is that you don't push the nozzle all the way up to the nipple.

To make the bubble baby, inflate an apple balloon about halfway and tie it off. Push the nozzle up inside the balloon and over to one side to the lower half of the balloon. Grab the knot from the outside with the other hand and remove your finger from the inside of the balloon (see illustration on the next page).

Twist the knot to form a little knob in the center of the balloon. This knob becomes the baby's nose. The natural bend in the bubble makes the cheeks, and a fold forms the mouth. To finish, all you need to do is draw in a pair of eyes.

CHINAMAN

The Chinaman is made in exactly the same way as the baby except that the knot is pushed up and connected to the upper half of the balloon. Twisting off the nose closer to the top of the head creates a more adult-shaped head and more pronounced folds in the balloon, giving its distinct appearance.

Mark eyes as shown, and you're finished.

BALDHEADED MAN

Inflate an apple balloon about halfway and tie it off. Twist off a small bubble next to the knot as shown below. Push the knot and the bubble up just as you did for the baby and the Chinaman. Grab it from the outside, remove your finger, and twist it off (the bubble not your finger).

By using a bubble you give your balloon guy a big bulbous nose. You'll notice that a mouth fold does not develop this time. Also, the head stretches, removing the dimple on top of it and making the green color blend into the rest of the balloon.

Draw in eyes and a mouth.

BUBBLES THE CLOWN

The clown is the same as the baldheaded man except that clown markings are added around the eyes and mouth.

MR. MUSTACHE

Mr. Mustache is made much like the bubble baby except that you use a penny or a small marble to form the nose.

Inflate an apple balloon as before. Place a penny on the knot and push both the penny and the knot inside the balloon. With the other hand grab the penny and the knot from the outside on the lower half of the balloon, remove the inside finger, and twist the penny to connect.

Your figure will have a large, but flat nose with several wrinkles under it, which look like whiskers. There will be no mouth fold, so you must draw the mouth in. Mark in the eyes and darken the mustache.

TROLL

This little creature is so gruesome that he's cute.

Begin the troll as you did Mr. Mustache, with a half inflated balloon and a penny. Push the penny and the knot inside the balloon, grabbing them from the outside with the other hand on the upper half of the balloon near where the green color begins. Twist to connect and form the nose.

Making the nose this far up the balloon forms a pronounced bend that produces many folds, including a frowning mouth fold. The nipple on top of the head moves down to the figure's forehead, forming a horn.

The addition of beady eyes and perhaps fangs, is all that's needed to complete this troll figure. Adorable! The kids will squeal . . . with delight.

SMILEY FACE

The smiley face has a striking resemblance to the comic-strip character Ziggy.

Inflate an apple balloon only about one-third this time, and tie it off. You need less air so you can form a more rounded head.

Use a marble or make a small bubble and push it all the way up into the nipple. Grab the bubble from the outside and twist to make the nose.

There is no mouth fold on this figure so you will need to draw in a smile. Finish by adding a couple of eyes.

MR. WRINKLE

Inflate an apple balloon halfway and tie it off. By using a penny you can give the nose a remarkably human shape. Push the penny up into the nipple. Position the penny inside the nipple at an angle. This will trap a small pocket of air. This is what gives it a human shape.

As you push the penny inside the balloon, bring the mouth fold close to the nose before twisting. This will stretch the back side of the head but will bunch the face, giving Mr. Wrinkle his wrinkles.

Draw on a pair of squinty eyes, and he's finished.

THE MASKED MARVEL

The Masked Marvel is the superhero of the balloon guys. Like all good superheros he wears a mask to hide his true identity.

You'll notice that the amount of green on the balloons varies from one balloon to the next; some balloons having more than others. In order to make the Masked Marvel you need to use a balloon with a substantial amount of green; this is what makes his mask. Use yellow and blue balloons because they seem to keep the color contrast during stretching better than the other colors.

If the balloon you're using has a large amount of green, you can insert the penny all the way to the tip of the nipple before twisting it off. If it has only a moderate amount of green you may position the penny on the side of the nipple rather than in the tip.

Twist to form the nose. A mouth fold should be present, so all you need to do is add eyes in the figure's "mask".

MORE BALLOON GUYS

A number of other faces can be made by varying the amount of air put into the balloon and the type of nose used. Chin size can be adjusted by moving the mouth closer or farther away from the nose before making the connecting twist. And of course, the markings you add can do a lot for creating character. Experiment and see what types of balloon guys you can create.

A few years ago a toy that was very popular with children was the Mad Ball, a rubber ball with a grotesque face. They're extremely ugly—I guess that's why they were so popular. With the stroke of your pen it's an easy task to transform a balloon guy into a horrible-looking Mad Ball, or more accurately a Mad Ball-oon.

Chapter 4

BALLOON HATS

BASIC BALLOON HAT

Balloon hats are easy to make and popular with kids. I'll describe how to make a basic hat and use that as the starting point for making a variety of styles.

Inflate a pencil balloon fully except for about two inches. Twist off a two-inch bubble. To determine the size of bubble 2, wrap the rest of the balloon around the head of the intended recipient. Remove the balloon and loop twist bubble 2, connecting points A and B. See the illustration on the following page.

The basic hat is now complete. With bubble 3 sticking up in back it takes on the appearance of an Indian headband and feather. Put this hat on your head—it will keep your "wig-wam".

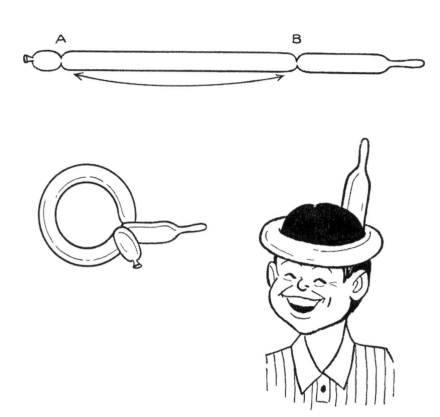

Turning the Indian hat upside down transforms it into a coonskin balloon cap. Add another balloon and you can make a variety of hats, such as the space helmet described below.

SPACE HELMET

Make the basic hat and set it aside. Take another pencil balloon and inflate it fully except for about an inch. Starting at the nozzle end, make the connections shown on the following page.

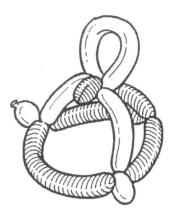

To make the antenna, squeeze the loop on top of the hat and twist it in half as shown. You're now finished.

ANIMAL HATS

First Hat

Make the basic balloon hat. With bubble 3 make a bird's head and beak in the same way you would make the swan's head. Finish by adding eyes.

Second Hat

Make the basic hat. Twist off bubble 3 into four bubbles (see the illustration on the following page). Connect points C and D. Bubble 3 becomes the animal's body, bubbles 4 and 5 his wings, and bubble 6 his head and nose. Add eyes and mouth.

Third Hat

This hat is made much like the previous one. From the basic hat take bubble 3 and squeeze the air down to eliminate the tail. Leave only a small nipple. This will make the balloon soft.

Make bubbles 3, 4, 5 and 6. Loop twist bubble 4 by connecting points C and D. Make a second loop twist around bubble 5 by connecting points D and E. This forms two ears. Bubble 6 becomes the animal's head. Add eyes and mouth.

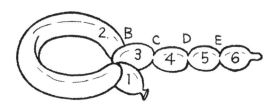

Fourth Hat

Start by making the basic hat. Take a second balloon and make any of the animals previously described (or even the airplane described in the next chapter). Twist connect the figure to the top of the "feather" bubble.

MULTIPLE BALLOON HAT

You will use two balloons to make this popular hat. Inflate a balloon leaving a four-inch tail. Measure the size of the recipient's head by wrapping the balloon around the head. If the balloon is too small, blown some more air into it. If you have already tied it off then squeeze it and force some air towards the tail.

Now twist off a one-inch bubble (1) and hold it. Divide the remaining portion of the balloon in half and make two bubbles (2 and 3). Twist off another one-inch bubble at the tail end (4). Connect points A and C. This forms the brim of the hat and should fit the recipient's head.

Take a second balloon and inflate it leaving a one-inch tail. Twist off a one-inch bubble at the nozzle end. Connect this bubble with point B on the first balloon. Twist off another one-inch bubble at the nipple end and connect it with point C on the first balloon. This makes the basic two-balloon hat. Place the hat on the recipient's head and you're finished.

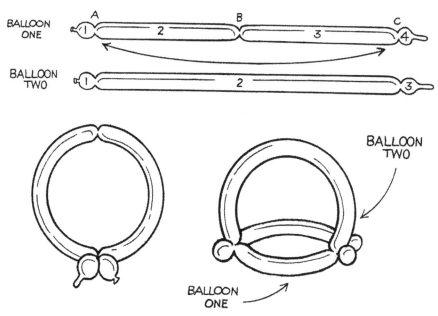

BALLOON ONE

BALLOON TWO

BALLOON TWO

BALLOON ONE

A variation of this hat is to add another balloon just like the second one. Connect it at the same points B and C. Adjust the air in the third balloon so it's length is the same as the second balloon. This way the hat remains symmetrical.

You can add more balloons if you wish to make a variety of hats. Use the basic two-balloon hat to start with and add on balloons at different locations and see what you can end up with.

ROYAL CROWN

You can become the king or queen of balloons with a balloon crown. The royal crown is a variation of the multiple balloon hat previously described and is made with three balloons. Start by making the basic two-balloon hat as described in the previously. Take a third balloon and attach it perpendicular to the second balloon.

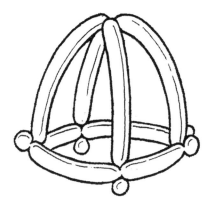

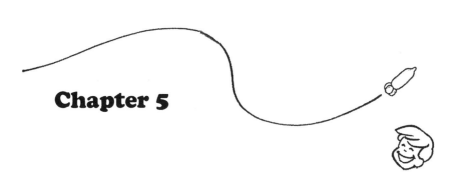

Chapter 5

TOYS AND GAMES

AIRPLANE

If an athlete gets athlete's foot, what do astronauts get? You guessed it—missile toe.

This fun toy balloon looks like the old doubled wing biplane of World War I. To make an airplane, inflate a balloon fully except for about two inches. Twist off a bubble, about two and a half inches long, this will be the plane's nose. Twist off two four-inch bubbles (2 and 3). Connect points A and B.

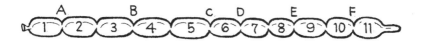

Twist off two more four-inch bubbles (4 and 5). Connect points B and C.

You're finished with the plane's front wings; now twist off a three-inch bubble (6) to form the central body segment.

Twist off two three-inch bubbles (7 and 8) and connect them at points D and E for one pair of rear wings. Do the same for bubbles 9 and 10 to finish the figure.

One last step makes the airplane easily recognizable and realistic—adding a propeller. To do this take a wooden match and break off and discard the match head. Keep the length of the match at least one and a half inches. Now insert the match inside the rim of the nozzle.

Push the match through the rubber so that it splits open just behind the outside rim. Make a hole on the other side and center the match. Your propeller is now in place, and your plane is finished. Now take the plane and buzz off!

HIGH-FLYERS

Although the airplane just described can't fly on its own power, here are some balloons that can.

Inflate a pencil balloon fully without tying it off and ask, "What's this balloon going to be?" After listening to all the responses say, "Nope!" Release the balloon letting it fly around the room, "It's a shooting star."

Flying balloons always excite kids—they even excite me (I guess that means that I'm really just an overgrown kid). Everyone will want to fly these balloons themselves. It makes a fun activity.

Spinner

A spinner can be made by curling the balloon as you inflate it. The best way to do this is to wrap it around a broom handle and have someone hold the balloon as you fill it with air. Remove the balloon. Now when you release your hold on the nozzle the balloon will twirl in the air—a dazzling sight!

Whistling Flyer

Cut a piece of stiff cardboard about 1/2 x 3/4 inches. After inflating the balloon insert the cardboard into the mouthpiece. Release the balloon and let it fly. The balloon will give off a loud whistle as it shoots around the room.

TULIP

To make a tulip, inflate a pencil balloon only one inch, just enough to make one medium-sized bubble, and then tie it off.

Take the nozzle and push it with one finger, inside the bubble all the way to the uninflated portion. Grab hold of the nozzle with the other hand and twist (apple twist) the bubble a couple of revolutions, locking the nozzle in place.

The tulip is now complete. Using different colored balloons you can make several, put them in a vase and have a bouquet. These flowers take very little care and never dry up or turn brown, although they will wilt after a few days.

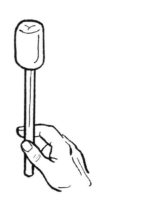

The Wilting Tulip

A tulip can be used as a fun game with kids. Tell everyone that the flower you created is magic, and can "smell." Its sense of smell is so good that it can identify those who ate fish-flavored Jello for lunch.

Hold the tulip with the thumb and first finger. Ask someone to blow on the flower. As he does so, pinch the stem lightly and push the thumb gently upward, making the movement as inconspicuous as possible. When you do this the flower will drop over, as if dead. Claim that the person must have eaten fish-flavored Jello for lunch.

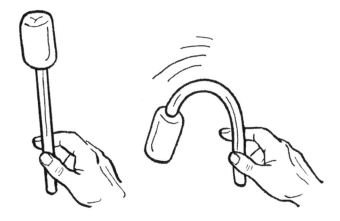

To "revive" the tulip, fan it with your free hand to give it fresh air. Release your grip on the stem slightly and shift the thumb down, allowing the flower to pop back up.

You can end this gag by blowing on it yourself with the tulip dropping over dead. Exclaim, "I don't understand it? I had a peanut butter and jelly sandwich for lunch. Say, come to think of it, the sandwich did taste a little peculiar. Maybe it was the jelly I used. It was a new flavor—the label on the jar said jelly-fish."

ELEPHANT NOSE

This is more of a gag than it is a balloon figure, but it's easy to make and gets a quick laugh.

Use a #245 pencil balloon or cut a #260 in half before starting. Inflate the balloon fully, leaving only about one half-inch uninflated.

Twist off two bubbles about one or two inches long. Ear twist bubble 2. If the balloon doesn't already have a natural curve, you can put one in by bending it. Now your balloon is complete. Just clamp bubbles 1 and 2 on your nose and you've become an elephant (or a Pinocchio). The kids will want to try this nose on for size.

You can make various sized noses depending on the size and shape of the balloon. This is a good way to use a broken piece of balloon.

CLOWN NOSE

Using an apple balloon you can make a bulbous clown nose. Inflate the balloon about halfway and twist off two small bubbles, one at each end of the balloon. Pull them together and twist connect them.

Clamp the two small bubbles onto your nose, and presto! You look as goofy as a clown.

 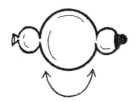

PIRATE SWORD

Kids love to play with swords. Here is a sword that's fun and safe. Inflate a pencil balloon fully except for about one inch. Twist off one two-inch bubble and one large bubble about 11 inches long. Twist connect points A and B. Bend bubble 3 back and through the loop of bubble 2. Bubble 2 becomes the hand guard and bubble 3 the blade.

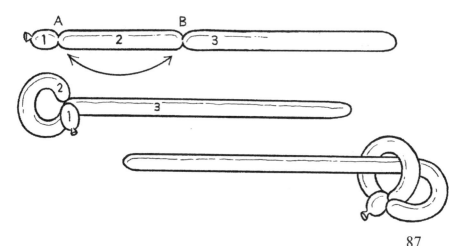

BUBBLE GUN

Here's a balloon gun that really works. The bullets are tiny balloons which you make. Let's start by making a bullet. Inflate a pencil balloon eight inches or more. Twist off a half-inch bubble. Now insert this bubble into the balloon, as shown in the illustration.

Use a pin and make a hole in the balloon behind the small bubble. Let all of the air out of the large balloon; the small balloon will remain inflated. Cut off the excess balloon, and your bullet is finished. The double wall on the small balloons makes these little bubbles very durable.

To make the gun, start by tying a knot in an uninflated balloon two inches from the nipple. Cut off the nipple end and discard. This is done merely to shorten the balloon. Inflate the balloon fully except for about a fourth of an inch, and tie it off.

Make the gun exactly the same way as the sword. Since you shortened the balloon, instead of a long sword blade you end up with a short gun barrel (see the illustration).

Push the bullet into the barrel of the gun. Grab the bullet with you trigger finger and thumb, and hold it until you're ready to fire. Shoot by aiming and releasing the bubble. The bullet can be harmlessly shot ten feet or more.

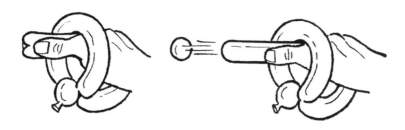

If you would like the bullet to go farther, add more weight to it. This can be done by inserting a small wad of paper into the balloon before making the bullet.

The gun can make exciting games for kids. Give each one a gun and some bullets and play shoot-'em-up or have a one on one shoot-out.

A fun activity is to have a contest to see who can shoot their bullets the farthest. This is tricker, and funnier, then it might sound. These bubbly projectiles are unpredictable and nearly uncontrollable, especially for beginners. You aim and shoot as best you can, but where the bullet goes is anybody's guess. It may shoot straight forward one time, curve far off to the right the next, or spiral upward or even behind the shooter, creating much amusement for the participants.

Another challenging and fun activity is similar to the playground game of dodge-ball, but using the balloon bubbles and guns instead of balls. Form a large ring of trigger happy kids around a single brave soul. The shooter whose bullet hits the player in the center of the ring first becomes the new target and has the fun of trying to evade all of the flying bubbles.

FEARLESS FREDDY

Fearless Freddy Fly Fighter (try saying that real fast five times) is a fun balloon game similar to pin the tail on the donkey. To play this game you need a big, ugly fly and several fly zappers.

Where do you find a big, ugly fly? No, you don't need to look in your garbage can. You will make one out of a balloon. You will also make the fly zappers.

Let's start with the fly. Blow up a pencil balloon, leaving about an inch uninflated. Burp the balloon to soften it, and then tie it off. Twist off one two-inch soft bubble (1) and two regular two-inch bubbles (2 and 3). You can make the first bubble a little softer than normal by squeezing some of the air out of it just before you twist it off. Connect points A and B.

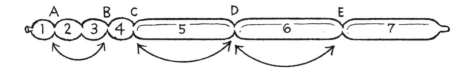

Twist off a one- to two-inch bubble (4) and a eight-inch bubble (5). Loop twist bubble 5, connecting points C and D.

Make bubble 6 the same size as bubble 5 and loop twist it, connecting points D and E. Bubbles 5 and 6 form the fly's wings, and the remaining bubble becomes the body.

Push bubble 1 about a fourth of the way between bubbles 2 and 3. Use your marker to draw two very large eyes on bubbles 2 and 3. Draw two dots on bubble 1 for the nose. Your fly is complete.

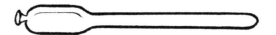

Each fly zapper is made with one pencil balloon.  Inflate the balloon fully, then release all the air leaving just enough to form a two- or three-inch bubble at the nozzle. Inflating the balloon first makes the zapper's tail larger and easy to see.

Make one fly zapper for each player and write the player's name on the bubble. Insert a straight pin into the nozzle of each zapper, as shown here.

You are now ready to play the game. Tape the monstrous fly on the wall at about shoulder level. The object of the game is to zap (pop) the fly with the fly zapper while blindfolded.

Each contestant in turn assumes the role of Fearless Freddy Fly Fighter, armed with a powerful fly zapper on a mission to rid the house of a giant, pesky fly.

Players are led one at a time to a spot several feet in front of the fly, and are blindfolded. Once the blindfold is in place, the player turns around several times to get slightly dizzy, and then is pointed toward the fly. Holding up the zapper, he or she walks toward the fly and sticks the pin into the wall (you can use tape instead of a pin if desired). When the players make contact with the wall the zapper loses its power and must remain where it landed until the game is over. Each player tires his or her skill until everyone has had a chance to be Fearless Freddy. The winner is the player whose zapper is closest to the fly, or who succeeds in popping it.

If someone pops the fly before all the players have had a turn a new fly is made and used. If two or more players happen to pop the fly, they must either share the prize or play one more time. If the fly was not destroyed, the winner (the one whose zapper was closest to the fly) has the privilege of popping the balloon without the blindfold and become the hero.

INDEX

Airplane, 81-82
Airship balloons, 7, 63
Animal hats, 776-78
Alligator, 58
Apple balloons, 7, 63-72

Baldheaded man, 67
Balloon care, 8-9
Balloon guys, 66-72
Balloonologist, 5
Balloon popping, 11
Balloon storage, 9
Bee body balloons, 7, 63
Brontosaurus, 41-43
Bubble baby, 65
Bubble gun, 88-90
Bubbles, 14-17
Bumblebee, 31-32

Camel, 27
Character aids, 17
Chinaman, 66-67
Clown, 68
Clown nose, 87
Cobra, 47
Cocker spaniel, 23
Color, 18
Connecting twists, 15

Dachshund, 22
Dog, 20-22
Dr. Dropo, 5-6

Ear Twist, 17
Elephant nose, 86
Extraterrestrial, 59-60

Fearless Freddy, 90-91
Felt tip marker, 18
French poodle, 43-46
Frog, 29-30
Fruit, 64-65

Giraffe, 24

Hats, 73-80
High-flyer, 83
Horse, 27
Hummingbird, 33

Inflation, 9-13

Ladybug, 33-34
Loop twist, 16

Masked Marvel, 71
Monkey, 54-55
Mouse, 25

Mr. Mustache, 68
Mr. Wrinkle, 70
Mugwump, 30-31
Multiple balloon hat, 79-80
Parrot, 49-50
Pen, 18
Pencil balloons, 7
Penguin, 38-40
Pumps, 10

Rabbit, 28
Royal crown, 80

Seal, 37-38
Smiley face, 69-70
Snail, 48
Space helmet, 74
Spinner, 83
Spots, 17
Squirrel, 26

Standing dog, 56-57
Stripes, 17
Swan, 35-36

Teddy bear, 61-62
Toucan, 50-52
Troll, 69
Tulip, 84
Twists, 14-17
Twistys, 7
Tying balloons
    first method, 13
    second method, 14
Tyrannosaurus rex, 52-53

Whiskers, 17
Whistling flyer, 84
Wilting tulip, 85
Wings, 31-32
Worm, 19

Resource Gallery

THE BIRTHDAY PARTY BUSINESS
How to Make A Living As A Children's Entertainer
By Bruce Fife, Hal Diamond, Steve Kissell, Robin Vogel, Mary Lostak, Bob Conrad, and Marcela Murad

Balloons, fun, games, magic, and more—they're all here. From entertaining and food to marketing and promotions, this book features comprehensive and detailed guidance on how to succeed in the birthday party business. You will find detailed information on entertaining children of all ages from preschoolers to adults. You will learn how to work with children, what they like, what they don't like, how to make them laugh, and how to control them. You will learn the secrets of entertaining using magic, clowning, puppetry, storytelling, ballooning, and face painting, as well as gain valuable information on catering, party games, and creating enchanting theme parties.

This book has everything you need to get started in the birthday party business; included are samples of advertisements, sales letters, thank you notes, news releases, contracts, party planning guides, flyers, business cards, stationery, giveaways, and more. Whether you are looking for a full-time profession that allows you to play for pay or are simply looking for a fun part-time avenue to make extra cash, this book, written by seven professional birthday party entertainers, will guide you every step of the way.

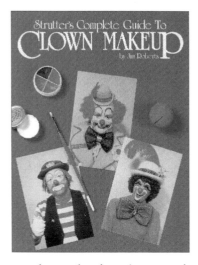

STRUTTER'S COMPLETE GUIDE TO CLOWN MAKEUP
By Jim "Strutter" Roberts

It takes know-how to create a professional looking clown face. Contrary to popular belief, a proper clown face is not warn as a mask. It should be designed to compliment the natural features in the face in order to enhance the clown's expressions. In this book an award winning clown describes in detail how to design a unique clown face of your own and how to properly apply makeup that will give your clown face that professional look.

Contains tips on powdering, applying rubber and putty noses, how to handle eyeglasses, solving common makeup problems, and proper makeup selection and removal. Profusely illustrated with over 100 full color photos. The information in this book is simple enough for beginners yet detailed enough for professional entertainers.

Provides detailed step-by-step directions for applying makeup to make each of the basic clown face types. The most complete and informative book ever written on clown makeup.

Visit us on the Web

Piccadilly Books, Ltd.

www.piccadillybooks.com

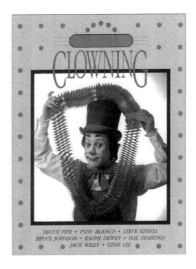

BRUCE FIFE • TONY BLANCO • STEVE KISSELL
BRUCE JOHNSON • RALPH DEWEY • HAL DIAMOND
JACK WILEY • GENE LEE

CREATIVE CLOWNING, 3rd Ed.
Edited and Compiled by
Bruce Fife
Foreword by
Richard Snowberg

The most concise, idea filled book on the art of clowning ever written. Every topic is covered in detail. "...a fun, amusing, thoroughly enjoyable book to read!"

—Ed Harris

"More than balloon tying and makeup tips, this tutorial teaches the practical and business aspects of the clowning profession. A history of clowning includes notes on famous entertainers and advice on developing a unique character. The eight authors, all experts in the field, explain the how-to's of juggling, puppetry, slapstick, magic, joke telling, and stilt walking. Even for those not aspiring to clown stardom or planning to set up their own entertainment business, this volume can be useful as a source for planning a party or special school event. Addresses for publications, organizations, and suppliers are appended."

—*Booklist*, American Library Association

"Included are chapters on how to be a birthday party clown, ideas for jobs, and a list of clown publications and organizations. The strengths of the book lie in the detailed, comprehensive coverage of the topic, the inclusion of many ideas and examples, and the emphasis on in-depth understanding of the process involved in creation of character and comic routine."

—*School Library Journal*

THE NUTTIEST, WACKIEST, FUNNIEST SKITS EVER!

By Stanley Snickelfoose

This book is packed with 50 of the most hilarious comedy skits ever! All of the skits are easy-to-perform and utilize two or more performers. Are they nutty? Unquestionably! Will audiences enjoy them? Definitely! Are they outrageously fun? Absolutely! These side-splitting comedy skits, are sure to tickle your funny bone and get you laughing out loud. Ideal for clowns, family entertainers, school performances, youth groups, or just for fun.

The author is a professional clown and children's entertainer with over twenty years experience amusing children and adults. With a name like Stanley Snickelfoose, you've got to be funny!

Visit us on the Web

P B Piccadilly Books, Ltd.

www.piccadillybooks.com

CLOWN MAGIC
By David Ginn

Clowning is fun. Magic is fun. Putting the two together doubles the fun and enjoyment. In this book you will learn how to effectively combine the humor and funny antics of clowning with the thrill and enchantment of magic. This is not simply a book about clowning, nor is it just a book of comedy magic tricks. It is a guide on how to be entertainingly funny using magical effects and silly stunts in a clownish way. Covers the theory of clown magic and practical applications, including hundreds of skits, routines, tricks, and gags. Written by award-winning magician and popular children's entertainer David Ginn. Includes contributions from Leon "Buttons" McBryde and many other professional clowns. A unique and entertaining text for those who are clowns at heart!

www.piccadillybooks.com

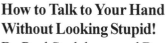

VENTRILOQUISM MADE EASY
How to Talk to Your Hand
Without Looking Stupid!
By Paul Stadelman and Bruce Fife

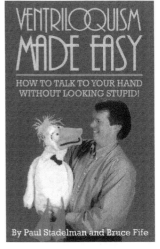

Lean how to throw your voice! Make your hand talk, your shoe sing, and your mother-in-law shut-up! Everyone will be tongue-tied when you start talking to the lamp shade—and it talks back!

Paul Stadelman, a professional ventriloquist who starred on his own television show for many years, shares with you the secrets that made him a hilarious success.

Ventriloquism, as taught in this book, is easy to learn if you follow a few simple rules. ANYBODY can do it. And it's so fun that once you start, you'll be talking to yourself for hours.

This book explains how to use standard puppets as well as novelty figures such as balloon animals and socks. Includes 22 complete comedy dialogues to get you started. All outrageously funny.

"An OUTSTANDING quality job...a fresh new look at a very popular form of entertainment."
—Stephen Axtell, Axtell Expressions

"Wonderful book!...the best resource book currently on the market for the aspiring ventriloquist."
—Clinton Detweiler, Director of Maher Ventriloquist Studies and President of The North American Association of Ventriloquists

"This is must reading for 'budding' ventriloquists."
—Robert H. Ladd, *Dialogue*

The Official Guide to the Nuttiest Sport Ever!
HOW TO BE A
GOOFY JUGGLER
A COMPLETE COURSE IN JUGGLING
MADE RIDICULOUSLY EASY!
By Bruce Fife

HOW TO BE A GOOFY JUGGLER
A Complete Course in Juggling Made Ridiculously Easy
By Bruce Fife

Juggle! Who can? You can. Anybody can learn to juggle. It's easy. It doesn't require great athletic skill or superior coordination. If you have the ability to roll out of bed in the morning, you have all the talent needed to become a wonderfully goofy juggler. Easy to follow instructions plus hundreds of juggling jokes and gags.

"Presented in a bright, witty tone, the book is pure fun...It's easy to read...and will definitely entertain you."
—*The Post Newspapers.*

"This is the kind of book I would like to have read when I first started to learn to juggle. It's easy to read with plenty of humor, jokes, and photos showing different types and styles of juggling."
—Roger Montandon, world renowned juggler

"If you want to do something weird, try *How to Be a Goofy Juggler*...which will make you giggle even if you are as butterfingered as I am...One thing guaranteed is a great time."
—Marilis Hornidge, *Book Bag Reviews*

Dr. Dropo's
JUGGLING BUFFOONERY
By Dr. Dropo

Here's a whole book jam-packed with comic juggling skits. Easy enough for beginners, funny enough for pros. This book will show you how to make your juggling hilariously funny. Most all of the juggling tricks are simple and easy to learn, some routines don't even require any real juggling, relying strictly on comedy dialogue and physical comedy.

"People who want to develop an act for birthday parties or street corners, but who don't know where to start, will find this book a blessing."
—*Juggler's World.*

Piccadilly Books, Ltd.
www.piccadillybooks.com

THE WORLD'S FUNNIEST CLOWN SKITS
By Barry DeChant

This book contains 50 of the most hilarious, high spirited, comedy clown skits of all time. The most popular new skits as well as classic favorites with new twists are included. Each of the skits have been carefully selected for ease in presentation and high audience appeal. Written and compiled by award-winning clown, Barry DeChant, a former president of the World Clown Association. He has brought together in one volume some of the funniest clown skits he has experienced during his many years as a professional entertainer and clown educator. Each of the skits is categorized for one, two, three, four, and more clowns, making this book a perfect resource for a solo performance or a group extravaganza.

Visit us on the Web

 Piccadilly Books, Ltd.

www.piccadillybooks.com

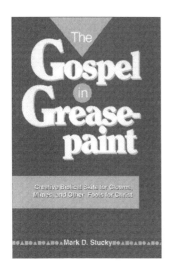

THE GOSPEL IN GREASEPAINT
Creative Biblical Skits for Clowns, Mimes, and Other Fools for Christ
By Mark D. Stucky

This book is packed with forty-two highly entertaining clown skits based on biblical themes. Children love clowns and clowns love children—so what better way to show God's love and teach His gospel than through clowns? All the skits are based on Bible stories and teach Christian ethics and morals in a way that is fun and entertaining.

Both adults and children will enjoy seeing as well as participating in these creative skits. No memorization is needed. All of the skits are presented in a variety of pantomime and acting situations with appropriate narration.

You can use these skits whenever you have a group of kids. Makes an ideal resource for clown and youth ministry groups. Clown skits provide an exciting way to teach Bible knowledge, encourage cooperation, build group unity, share the gospel with others, and have fun!

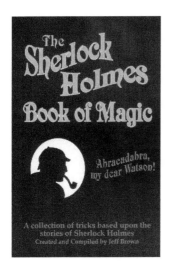

SHERLOCK HOLMES BOOK OF MAGIC A Collection of Tricks Based Upon the Stories of Sherlock Holmes
by Jeff Brown

"Solid material...This is an excellent way, at a bargain price, for a newcomer to learn and to present good magic...Highest recommendation."
—*The Linking Ring*.

The stories of Sherlock Holmes have inspired this collection of magical effects designed to baffle your friends, entertain your audience, and stimulate their imaginations. You will be able to thrill and delight your audiences in a way unlike other magicians. Although Holmes never admitted to having magical powers, his ability to solve crimes bordered on the supernatural. Now you can combine the thrill and excitement of magic with the mystery and suspense of a spine-tingling Sherlock Holmes mystery.

But beware—this collection of magic tricks is not recommended for the faint of heart. These tricks are guaranteed to amaze, amuse, enlighten, and dumbfound your audience. Everyone will be in total shock when you magically solve each crime. As Holmes might have said, "Abracadabra, my dear Watson. The magic show is afoot!"

"What a delightful book!...I give this a four pipe rating out of four pipes and heartily recommend it to be added to your magic library. Ten dollars is so low, it is almost criminal."
—Michael Tulkoff, Society of American Magicians.

HOLDING AUDIENCE ATTENTION
How to Speak with Confidence, Substance, and Power
By L. Perry Wilbur

Have you ever listened to a dynamic speaker or performer who immediately aroused the audience's attention and kept them spellbound for the entire presentation? How do they do it? What is their magic formula? In this book you will learn the secrets used by professional speakers and actors to quickly grab and hold an audience's attention. You will learn how to speak and act with confidence, substance, and power.

Whether you are simply giving a talk at a local meeting or have goals of becoming a paid speaker or performer this book will show you how to present yourself and your material like a seasoned professional.

L. Perry Wilbur is the author of 25 books and thousands of articles. He is a former advertising copywriter, consultant, and university instructor.

Visit us on the Web

Piccadilly Books, Ltd.
www.piccadillybooks.com